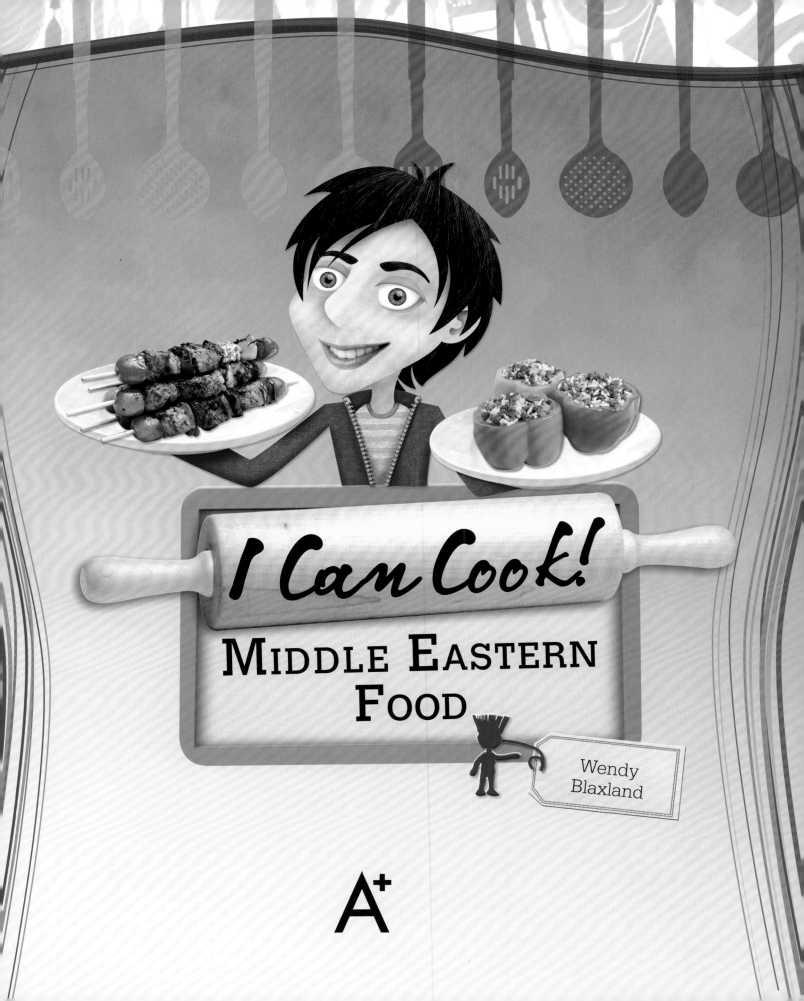

I Can Cook!

MIDDLE EASTERN FOOD

Wendy Blaxland

A+

Smart Apple Media
P.O. Box 3263
Mankato, MN, 56002

First published in 2011 by
MACMILLAN EDUCATION AUSTRALIA PTY LTD
15–19 Claremont St, South Yarra, Australia 3141

Visit our website at www.macmillan.com.au or go directly to www.macmillanlibrary.com.au

Associated companies and representatives throughout the world.

Copyright text © Wendy Blaxland 2011

Library of Congress Cataloging-in-Publication Data

Blaxland, Wendy.
   Middle Eastern food / Wendy Blaxland.
       p. cm. — (I can cook!)
   Includes index.
   Summary:"Describes historical, cultural, and geographical factors that have influenced the cuisine of the Middle East.
   Includes recipes to create Middle-Eastern food"—Provided by publisher.
   ISBN 978-1-59920-672-1 (library binding)
   1. Cooking, Middle Eastern—Juvenile literature. 2. Food—Middle East—History—Juvenile literature. 3. Cookbooks. I. Title.
   TX725.M628B58 2012
641.5956—dc22
                          2011005450
Publisher: Carmel Heron
Commissioning Editor: Niki Horin
Managing Editor: Vanessa Lanaway
Editor: Laura Jeanne Gobal
Proofreaders: Georgina Garner; Kirstie Innes–Will
Designer: Stella Vassiliou
Page Layout: Stella Vassiliou
Photo Researcher: Claire Armstrong (management: Debbie Gallagher)
Illustrators: Jacki Sosenko; Guy Holt (map, **7**, **9**); Gregory Baldwin (map icons, **9**)
Production Controller: Vanessa Johnson

Manufactured in China by Macmillan Production (Asia) Ltd.
Kwun Tong, Kowloon, Hong Kong
Supplier Code: CP March 2011

Acknowledgments
The author would like to thank the following for their generous help and expert advice: Emeritus Professor Eugene Anderson, University of California; Wayne Olson, Reference Librarian, U.S. National Agricultural Library; Lynne Olver, editor, FoodTimeline; Dena Saulsbury-Monaco, cook and librarian, Montreal.

The author and the publisher are grateful to the following for permission to reproduce copyright material:

Front cover photographs: Stuffed peppers courtesy of iStockphoto.com/DreamBigPhotos; Turkish delight courtesy of Shutterstock/Ilker Canikligil; shish kebabs courtesy of Shutterstock/Martin Darley; orange juice in glass courtesy of Shutterstock/happydancing.
Back cover photographs: Brown paper bag courtesy of Shutterstock/Nils Z; hummus courtesy of Shutterstock/bonchan; figs courtesy of Shutterstock/Oliver Hoffmann; cucumbers courtesy of Shutterstock/Nataly Lukhanina; eggplants courtesy of Shutterstock/Nattika; pomegranates courtesy of Shutterstock/Valentyn Volkov; and parsley courtesy of Shutterstock/Volosina.

Photographs courtesy of: Corbis/S Sabawoon, **29**, /Viel/SoFood, **15** (top left); Dreamstime/Igordutina, **6** (almonds), /Looby, **7** (top center); Getty Images/ Khaled Desouki, **28** (bottom), /Dennis Gottlieb, **23** (chicken couscous), /Ramzi Haidar, **28** (top), /Images Of Africa, **19** (tabouli), /Abid Katib, **5** (bottom right); iStockphoto.com/ajafoto, **10** (tea towel), /brinkstock, **13** (clipboard), /Floortje, **7** (center right), /Irochka_T, **4** (ice), **25** (ice), /jokerproduction, **6** (basket), /kkgas, **30** (center), /Robyn Mac, **10** (hanging utensils), /Urosh Petrovic, **throughout** (red oven mitt), /SensorSpot, **4** (boy); Photolibrary/Steve Brown, **27** (top left), /A Demotes, **7** (bottom right), /Andre Martin, **21** (bottom left); Shutterstock/Afonkin_Y, **8** (barley), /aliisik, **26** (Turkish delight), **27** (Turkish delight), /Aaron Amat, **11** (grater), /AntoinetteW, **22** (couscous), **23** (couscous), /Mark Aplet, **13** (electric mixer), /Arkady, **8** (pita), /artproem, **8** (fish), /atoss, **8** (prawns), /Marilyn Barbone, **8** (saffron), /Roxana Bashyrova, **8** (green & black grapes), /Mircea Bezergheanu, **8** (dates), /bonchan, **17** (hommus), /Nikola Bilic, **18** (parsley), **19** (flat parsley), /Adrian Britton, **10** (baking tray), /Darren Brode, **11** (electric mixer), /Ilker Canikligil, **10** (saucepan), **13** (saucepan), /carla720, **8** (couscous), /ZH Chen, **10** (measuring cups), /Coprid, **13** (soap dispenser), /Mikael Damkier, **10** (frying pan, measuring jug), /ejwhite, **11** (colander), /Raphael Daniaud, **11** (blender), /Elena Elisseeva, **8** (mint), **9** (wheat), **24** (mint), **25** (mint), /EuToch, **21** (skewers), /f/stop, **7** (center left), /Faraways, **7** (top left), /Iakov Filimonov, **13** (knives), /Angelo Giampiccolo, **30** (bottom), /Gilmanshin, **13** (knife block), /Givaga, **9** (prawns), /grublee, **15** (tomatoes), **18** (tomatoes), **19** (halved tomatoes), **21** (tomatoes), /Eva Gruendemann, **7** (bottom left), /Hal_P, **14** (capsicum), **15** (capsicums), **20** (capsicums), **21** (capsicums), **23** (capsicums), /happydancing, **25** (orange sharbat), /Oliver Hoffmann, **6** (figs), /Jiang Hongyan, **8** (coriander), /Iorga Studio, **8** (lamb), /Alexandar Iotzov, **9** (rice), /Tischenko Irina, **10** (large knife, butter knife), /Eric Isselée, **9** (goat), /Luis Carlos Jimenez del rio, **9** (olives), /Joat, **30** (top), /K13 ART, **8** (blue bowls, green bowls), **11** (bowls), /Kayros Studio, **13** (fire extinguisher), **31**, /Vitaly Korovin, **8** (tomatoes), **19** (whole tomatoes), /Wolfe Larry, **8** (red grapes), /LazarevDN, **10** (sieve), /Chris Leachman, **10** (chopping board), /Lepas, **8** (feta), /Loskutnikov, **8** (dates), /Nataly Lukhanina, **8** (cucumbers), /Nattika, **9** (citrus fruit), /Milos Luzanin, **9** (fish), /Petr Malyshev, **13** (kettle), /Ivan Montero Martinez, **16** (chickpeas), **17** (pale chickpeas), /Marco Mayer, **17** (chickpeas & spoon), /Iain McGillivray, **10** (tongs), /mimo, **24** (oranges), /Mopic, **13** (first-aid box), /John Nairne, **8** (onions), /Irina Nartova, **26** (rose petals), **27** (rose petals), /Denis Nata, **4** (oranges), **5** (oranges), **25** (orange slices), /Nattika, **8** (eggplants), /Fedorov Oleksiy, **8** (garlic), /Picsfive, **9** (sardines), /Ragnarock, **11** (slotted spoon), **13** (frying pan), /Stephen Aaron Rees, **11** (wooden spoon), /Elena Schweitzer, **8** (watermelon), /SMARTPics, **8** (rice), /soncerina, **10** (fork), /STILLFX, **10** (peeler), /svry, **7** (top right), /Ev Thomas, **13** (fire blanket), /Tobik, **8** (yoghurt), /ultimathule, **8** (figs), /Matt Valentine, **10** (bread knife), /Velychko, **9** (milk products), /Graça Victoria, **10** (oven mitts), **13** (oven mitts), /Vlue, **10** (steak knife), /Valentyn Volkov, **4** (pomegranates), **5** (pomegranates), **8** (pomegranates), **9** (grapes), /Volosina, **8** (parsley), /Voronin76, **8** (chicken), /FengYu, **8** (lemons), **16** (lemons); Brenda Smith, **7** (bottom center).

While every care has been taken to trace and acknowledge copyright, the publisher tenders their apologies for any accidental infringement where copyright has proved untraceable. They would be pleased to come to a suitable arrangement with the rightful owner in each case.

Contents

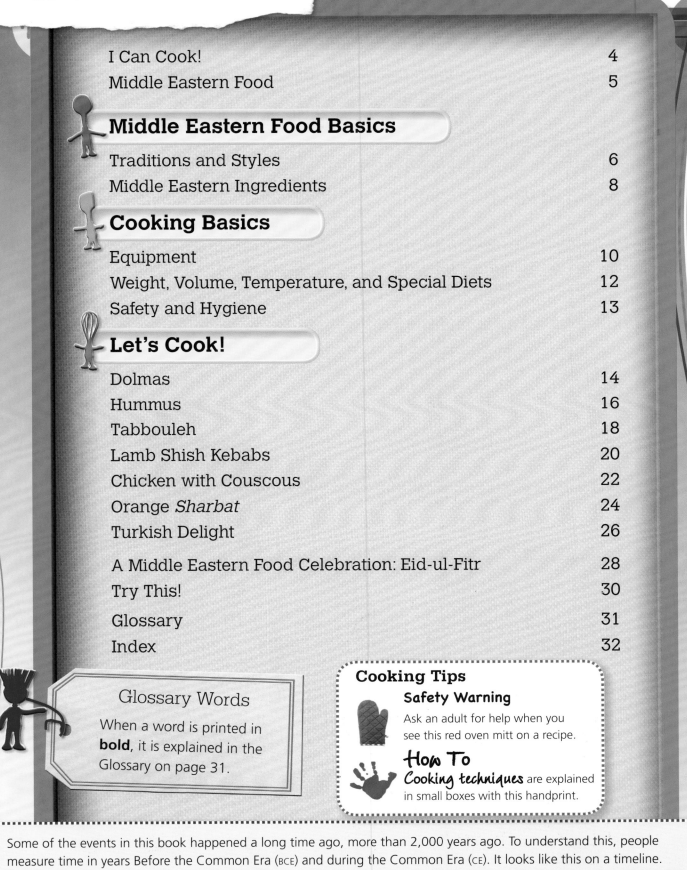

Glossary Words

When a word is printed in **bold**, it is explained in the Glossary on page 31.

Cooking Tips

Safety Warning

Ask an adult for help when you see this red oven mitt on a recipe.

How To

Cooking techniques are explained in small boxes with this handprint.

Some of the events in this book happened a long time ago, more than 2,000 years ago. To understand this, people measure time in years Before the Common Era (BCE) and during the Common Era (CE). It looks like this on a timeline.

| 150 | 100 | 50 | 0 | 50 | 100 | 150 |

Years BCE   Years CE

I Can Cook!

Cooking is a rewarding and lifelong skill. With some basic cooking knowledge, a little practice, and great recipes, you can cook entire meals! Cooking for your family and friends is a fun activity, and a mouthwatering meal can take you to places that you have never been. Are you ready to have fun cooking—and eating?

A World of Food

Every day, people all over the world cook delicious and **nutritious** meals. What they cook depends not only on the ingredients available to them, but also on their country's food **culture** or cooking style. A country's style of cooking is shaped over time by its culture, **economy**, **climate**, and the land itself.

Cook Your Way Around the World

You can explore the great cuisines of the world in your own kitchen. The special flavors and wonderful aromas of a country's food culture come from fresh ingredients and particular spices or herbs, which you can find in your local supermarket or a specialty store. Share with your family and friends authentic dishes from different countries that look great and taste even better.

You can cook mouthwatering food from different countries by following a few simple steps. Some recipes involve combining just a couple of ingredients!

4

Middle Eastern Food

Middle Eastern food refers to the delicious food cooked by people living in the countries surrounding the Persian Gulf and some Northern African countries. It blends local ingredients with European, Indian, and other Asian influences to create unique flavors.

Flavors of the World

Though the countries of the Middle East all have distinctive dishes, there are many common ingredients and cooking styles. These include the use of wheat, barley, garlic, lemon, and parsley, along with dates, nuts, and spices. All of these ingredients help to create healthy, satisfying, and aromatic foods. Tabbouleh, shish kebab and pilaf are well-known Middle Eastern dishes.

Cooking Middle Eastern Food At Home

You can cook a Middle Eastern dinner for your family easily at home. How about a simple couscous dish, followed by a tangy orange *sharbat* for dessert? This book has seven recipes that you can follow to cook a meal on your own or with a little help from an adult. Some of the recipes don't even involve cooking! The recipes can be adapted to suit special **diets**, too.

NORTH AMERICA

MIDDLE EAST

EUROPE

ASIA

AFRICA

SOUTH AMERICA

AUSTRALIA

N

The Middle East is a group of countries to the south and east of the Mediterranean Sea.

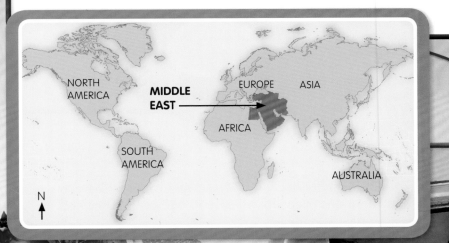

Sharbat, or sherbet, is a Middle Eastern summer favorite. Unlike the sherbet known in Western cultures, sharbat is a drink rather than a frozen dessert.

5

Middle Eastern Food Basics

Traditions and Styles

The Middle East is located between Europe, Asia, and Africa. Over many centuries, great **civilizations** have built the foundation of Middle Eastern cooking **traditions** and styles, including the Mesopotamian civilizations and the Persian and Ottoman **empires**. Traders also brought ingredients from Asia, Africa, and Europe to the Middle East.

Dates (left), figs (center), and almonds (right) are **native** to this area and commonly used in Middle Eastern cooking.

The Birth of Middle Eastern Food

The first civilizations in the world to grow wheat developed in an area called Mesopotamia (modern-day Iraq), between the Tigris and Euphrates rivers, for at least 10,000 years. They also used **staple foods** such as barley, pistachios, figs, and dates.

Between 550 BCE and 330 BCE, the Persian Empire ruled the area, adding rice, poultry, and fruit to Middle Eastern food. The wandering Bedouin desert peoples introduced meat stews, dairy products, grapes, almonds, and coffee, and Arab traders brought back exotic spices from Asia.

Later Influences

The arrival of the Ottomans (1200s–1800s CE) also saw the introduction of rice pilafs and honey-flavored sweets. North African foods, such as couscous, common in Morocco and Algeria, spread to the Middle East and, from the 1600s CE, new foods from the Americas, such as tomatoes and beans, were introduced through Europe. During the 1900s CE, **Jews** settling in Israel brought dumplings and other northern European foods.

Regional Food

Certain flavors, ingredients, and cooking methods are common throughout the Middle East. However, every country has its own specialties or a twist on favorite dishes. The map below shows some of the countries that make up the Middle East and discusses the ingredients and special foods that are popular in each.

Middle Eastern Sweets

The distinctive ingredients of Middle Eastern sweets are honey, nuts, and floral essences. Baklava is a pastry filled with chopped nuts and drenched in honey. Slivers of pistachio top crunchy toffee in *sohan* and soft Turkish delight is often flavored with rose water.

Turkey

Small *meze* (appetizer) dishes begin meals of lamb and chicken kebabs, sausages, and stews, along with bread and rice. Thick, strong Turkish coffee or cinnamon-scented tea (pictured) is served afterward. Popular street food includes pizza-like *pide*, bread rings, and chestnuts.

Iraq

Iraqi cooking is known for dolmas (stuffed or wrapped vegetables, pictured) and *masgouf* (grilled spicy fish).

Iran

Persian rice with lamb, chicken, or fish is served with vegetables and many types of flatbread. Fresh or dried fruit, such as plums, apricots, pomegranates, and quince, are popular. Persian ice cream (pictured) and pastries are typically flavored with rose water, mint, and cinnamon.

Syria and Lebanon

Kibbe (ground meat and crushed wheat patties or rolls) is a Syrian specialty. Lebanese food is often flavored with lemon and garlic, and includes spicy kofta (lamb meatballs) and baba ganoush (eggplant dip, pictured).

Israel

Israelis whose families have always lived in the Middle East cook spicy, aromatic dishes. However, Jewish people who have **migrated** recently from northern Europe enjoy sweeter recipes, including blintzes (pancakes, pictured) and honey candies.

Egypt

In Egypt, falafels (spicy bean patties, pictured) are as popular as creamy chicken *faateh*.

Gulf States

Indian spices are widely used in the Gulf State countries because of a large Indian migrant population. Seafood, such as shrimp, lobster, and fish, is popular, as are lentils. For dessert, custard with cardamom rose water (pictured) is a favorite.

Yemen

Yemeni cooking uses spicy mixtures such as *hawajat* and the chili and garlic-based *z'hug*. The national Yemeni dish, *saltah* (a spicy meat stew eaten with flatbread, pictured), was influenced by Ottoman Turkish cuisine.

Map labels:
Black Sea · TURKEY · Caspian Sea · Mediterranean Sea · SYRIA · LEBANON · JORDAN · ISRAEL · IRAQ · IRAN · KUWAIT · Persian Gulf · BAHRAIN · QATAR · EGYPT · SAUDI ARABIA · UNITED ARAB EMIRATES · GULF STATES · OMAN · Red Sea · SUDAN · ERITREA · YEMEN

Middle Eastern Food Basics

Middle Eastern Ingredients

Cooks in the Middle East serve bread or rice with every meal and use a variety of fresh produce. Important flavorings include spices such as cinnamon, saffron, nutmeg, cumin, and sumac, along with tamarind, onion, garlic, parsley, cilantro, and mint.

Meat

Lamb and chicken are commonly used in Middle Eastern cooking. Pork is rarely used because of Jewish and **Muslim** dietary rules. Beef is seldom eaten because cattle are rarely kept.

Seafood

Fish and other seafood, such as small, sweet shrimp, feature in coastal recipes.

Dairy Products

Cheese and yogurt are commonly used, especially in inland areas.

Fruit

The warm Middle East is suited to growing fruit. Watermelons, grapes, dates, figs, and pomegranates are popular. Citrus fruit, such as lemons, add a characteristic tang to Middle Eastern food.

Staple Foods

Bread and rice are staple foods in the Middle East. Semolina, which is made into couscous, and barley, used in dishes such as *kashkak* (a meat and barley stew), are also popular.

Vegetables

Commonly used vegetables include eggplant, cucumber, and tomato.

8

Landscapes and Climates

The Middle East is close to several seas and gulfs. Though this region is generally very dry and includes large desert areas, it is also home to **fertile** river valleys. Just like the landscape, the climate of this region varies widely as well, which means many different ingredients can be grown here. The map below shows which areas of the region the Middle East's produce comes from.

Olive oil comes from Jordan, Syria, and Turkey.

Wheat is grown in a few countries only, such as Turkey, Iran, and Iraq.

The long coastlines around the Mediterranean Sea and the Red Sea provide seafood, including mullet, sardines, and shrimp.

Middle Eastern countries with fertile agricultural land, such as Turkey, Iran, and Iraq, grow tomatoes, cucumbers, potatoes, and green vegetables. They also produce citrus fruit, grapes, figs, and melons. Egypt grows dates.

The rivers and lakes in the region also provide fish, such as trout and salmon.

Rice is grown in the north of Iran and in the lower Nile valley in Egypt.

Farmers raise cattle in Egypt, Iraq, and Yemen, sheep in Egypt, Iraq, and Israel, and goats in Israel and Jordan.

Different countries produce milk products, especially Saudi Arabia.

Black Sea · TURKEY · Caspian Sea · SYRIA · LEBANON · IRAQ · IRAN · ISRAEL · JORDAN · KUWAIT · BAHRAIN · Persian Gulf · QATAR · UNITED ARAB EMIRATES · EGYPT · SAUDI ARABIA · Red Sea · GULF STATES · OMAN · ERITREA · YEMEN · SUDAN

Equipment

Having the right equipment to cook with is very important. Here are some of the most common items needed in the kitchen.

Potato mashers break up food.

Sieves separate and break up food.

Spatulas lift and turn food.

Cook pasta, rice, soups, and stews in saucepans.

Big knives chop. Small knives cut and peel. Butter knives spread. Serrated knives slice.

Oven mitts protect hands from heat.

Baking pans hold food in an oven.

Forks hold, stir, or prick food.

Whisks beat food to add air and make it light.

Tongs are used to handle hot food.

Measuring cups and spoons measure ingredients accurately.

Frying pans fry or brown food.

Peelers remove the skins from fruit and vegetables.

Cutting boards provide safe surfaces for cutting food.

Blenders chop ingredients, mix food, and make smooth sauces and soups.

Spoons mix and stir. Wooden spoons prevent scratched pans. Slotted spoons let liquid drain away.

Graters shave thin slices from food, such as cheese.

Colanders drain liquids.

Mixers mix food quickly.

Bowls hold food for mixing.

Cooking Basics

Weight, Volume, Temperature, and Special Diets

It is important to use the right amount of ingredients, cook at the correct heat, and be aware of people with special dietary needs.

Weight and Volume

The weight and volume of ingredients can be measured with a weighing scale or with measuring cups and spoons. Convert them using this table. Measure dry ingredients so that they are level across the top of the spoon or cup without packing them down.

Recipe Measurement	Weight	Volume
1 cup	8 ounces	250 ml
½ cup	4 ounces	125 ml
2 tablespoons	1 ounce	30 ml
1 teaspoon	0.16 ounce	4.7 ml

Temperature

Fahrenheit and Celsius are two different ways of measuring temperature. Oven dials may show the temperature in either Fahrenheit or Celsius. Use lower temperatures in gas or convection ovens.

Oven Temperature	Celsius	Fahrenheit
Slow	150°	300°
Moderately slow	160°–170°	320°–340°
Moderate	180°	350°
Moderately hot	190°	375°
Hot	200°	400°
Very hot	220°–240°	430°–470°

Special Diets

Some people follow special diets because of personal or religious beliefs about what they should eat. Others must not eat certain foods because they are **allergic** to them.

Diet	What It Means	Symbol
Allergy-specific	Some people's bodies react to a certain food as if it were poison. They may die from eating even a tiny amount of this food. Nuts, eggs, milk, strawberries, and even chocolate may cause allergic reactions.	
Halal	Muslims eat only food prepared according to strict religious guidelines. This is called halal food.	
Kosher	Jews eat only food prepared according to strict religious guidelines. This is called kosher food.	
Vegan	Vegans eat nothing from animals, including dairy products, eggs, and honey.	
Vegetarian	Vegetarians eat no animal products and may or may not eat dairy products, eggs, and honey.	

Safety and Hygiene

Be safe in the kitchen by staying alert and using equipment correctly when cooking. Practicing good food hygiene means you always serve clean, germ-free food. Follow the handy tips below!

Be Organized

Hungry? Organized cooks eat sooner! First, read the recipe. Next, take out the equipment and ingredients you'll need and follow the stages set out in the recipe. Straighten up and clean as you go. While your food cooks, wash up, sweep the kitchen floor, and empty the garbage.

Heat

Place boiling saucepans toward the back of the stove with handles turned inward. Keep your hands and face away from steam and switch hot equipment off as soon as you have finished using it. Use oven mitts to pick up hot pots and put them down on heatproof surfaces. Always check that food is cool enough to eat.

Emergencies

All kitchens should have a fire blanket, fire extinguisher, and first-aid box.

Food Hygiene

To avoid spreading germs, wash your hands well and keep coughs and sneezes away from food. Use fresh ingredients and always store food that spoils easily, such as meat and fish, in the refrigerator.

Electricity

Use electrical equipment only with an adult's help. Switch the power off before unplugging any equipment and keep it away from water.

Knives

When cutting food with a knife, cut away from yourself and onto a nonslip surface, such as a suitable cutting board.

Let's Cook!

Dolmas

Stuffed vegetables probably developed from early Arab cooking styles. They were perfected by the Ottoman Turks and became popular all over the Middle East. Now, vegetables are either stuffed with meat and grains, and served hot with a sauce, or stuffed with rice, enriched with nuts, raisins, or beans, and served cold with oil. They are a great way of using young vegetables in late summer.

Equipment

- Wooden spoon
- Small bowl
- Small, sharp knife
- Cutting board
- Tablespoon
- Covered casserole dish
- Measuring cup

Ingredients

- 9 ounces of ground lamb (or lean beef)
- 1 tablespoon of olive oil
- ½ of an onion
- ¼ cup of finely chopped parsley
- A pinch of ground cinnamon
- ¼ teaspoon of freshly grated nutmeg
- ¼ teaspoon of ground allspice
- Freshly ground pepper, to taste
- 1½ cups of cooked rice
- 6 small vegetables that can be stuffed (try zucchini, tomato, or bell pepper)
- 3–5 rinsed cabbage leaves
- 2 cups of water
- 4 ounces of tomato paste
- Juice of half a lemon
- ½ cup of plain unsweetened yogurt

What to Do

1. Mix the ground meat with the oil, onion, parsley, cinnamon, nutmeg, allspice, pepper, and cooked rice in the small bowl, and place it in the refrigerator.

2. Cut the top off each vegetable carefully and use the tablespoon to scrape out most of the flesh and any seeds. Throw these away.

3. Line the casserole dish with cabbage leaves. Mix the water with the tomato paste and lemon juice. Pour this mixture into the casserole dish.

Ask an adult for help with using the knife and stove.

4

Stuff each vegetable with the rice and meat mixture. Place the vegetables upright in the casserole dish. Do not pack them too tightly. If there are too many vegetables, layer them using cabbage leaves between each layer. Cover the last layer with cabbage leaves.

5

Cover the casserole dish and heat it on low to medium heat until the meat is cooked and the vegetables are tender (about 20–25 minutes). If the dish starts to dry, gently add more water.

6

Take the casserole dish off the stove. Dolmas can be served hot, warm, or cold. Serve with a dollop of cold, unsweetened yogurt on the side.

Hummus

Hummus is a dip made from chickpeas that is popular throughout the Middle East. Ingredients in this dish, such as sesame seeds and garlic, were first used in Middle Eastern cooking thousands of years ago. Chickpeas have been eaten for more than 10,000 years! Hummus is a tasty, healthy, and protein-packed dip.

MAKES: 4–6 servings

PREPARATION TIME: 10 minutes

FOOD VALUES: About 60 calories, 4 g of fat, 2 g of protein, and 4 g of carbohydrates per serving.

SPECIAL DIETS: Suitable for vegan, vegetarian, nut-free, gluten-free, kosher, and halal diets.

Equipment

- Colander
- Cutting board
- Small, sharp knife
- Citrus juicer
- Blender (or potato masher)
- Serving bowl and plate

Ingredients

- 1½ cans of chickpeas (about 1½ pounds)
- 2 lemons
- 2 cloves of garlic
- 3 tablespoons of tahini (a sesame paste)
- A pinch of salt
- Mild, sweet, or spicy paprika, to taste
- 1 tablespoon of olive oil
- A few sprigs of parsley, finely chopped
- Pita bread

What to Do

1 Drain and wash the chickpeas in a colander. Reserve some of the liquid from the cans for later use.

2 Roll each lemon on the cutting board with the palm of your hand, pressing down hard to free the juice inside. Cut the lemons in half and squeeze the juice out with the citrus juicer.

3 Crush the garlic cloves lightly with the flat side of the knife. Peel the skin off and throw it away.

Ask an adult for help with using the knife and blender.

4 Put the chickpeas, lemon juice, tahini, crushed garlic, and salt in the blender and blend until a smooth paste forms. Add some of the reserved liquid if necessary for a soft, creamy texture.

5 Transfer the hummus to a serving plate and **garnish** with a sprinkle of paprika, a drizzle of olive oil, and a little chopped parsley. Serve with fresh pita bread.

Let's Cook!

MAKES: 4 servings

PREPARATION TIME: 15 minutes

FOOD VALUES: About 80 calories, 1 g of fat, 3 g of protein, and 11 g of carbohydrates per serving.

SPECIAL DIETS: Suitable for vegan, vegetarian, nut-free, gluten-free, kosher, and halal diets.

Tabbouleh

Tabbouleh comes from the mountains of Lebanon and it is now one of the world's most popular salads. Its base is parsley, which is very high in vitamin C. Tabbouleh means "little spicy," and it is served in the Middle East as part of the *meze* before the main meal. Try it at your next party!

Equipment

- Small bowl
- Small, sharp knife
- Cutting board
- Citrus juicer
- Sieve
- Medium-size bowl
- Wooden spoon
- Serving plate

Ingredients

- ½ cup of bulgur wheat
- 3 ripe tomatoes
- 1 lemon
- 2 cups of parsley, finely chopped
- Small sprig of mint, finely chopped
- 1 clove of garlic, finely chopped
- ½ of a red onion, finely chopped
- 1 tablespoon of extra virgin olive oil
- Salt, to taste
- 4 large rinsed lettuce leaves

What to Do

1 Put the bulgur wheat in the small bowl and fill the bowl with water to about ½ inch above the wheat. Soak the wheat for 15 minutes.

2 Cut the cores from the tomatoes, throw the cores away, then cut the tomatoes into small to medium cubes.

3 Roll the lemon on the cutting board with the palm of your hand, pressing down hard to free the juice inside. Cut the lemon in half and squeeze the juice out with the citrus juicer.

Recipe Variations

Add a tablespoon of toasted sesame seeds for extra flavor.

Try using couscous in the salad instead of bulgur wheat.

Ask an adult for help with using the knife.

Drain all of the water from the bulgur wheat using the sieve.

Combine all of the ingredients, apart from the lettuce leaves, in the medium-size bowl and mix well. Taste the tabbouleh and season with salt as necessary.

Transfer the tabbouleh to the serving plate and serve with lettuce leaves to use as scoops.

MAKES: 4 servings

PREPARATION TIME: 35 minutes

COOKING TIME: 5–10 minutes

FOOD VALUES: About 130 calories, 7 g of fat, 13 g of protein, and 2 g of carbohydrates per shish kebab.

SPECIAL DIETS: Suitable for nut-free and gluten-free diets. For vegan and vegetarian diets, replace the meat with vegetables or marinated tofu; and for kosher and halal diets, use certified meat.

Lamb Shish Kebabs

Shish kebabs are skewers of grilled meat that originated in Turkey. Lamb is traditionally used, but beef, goat, chicken, and pork may also be used, as well as seafood. Vegetables, such as onions, tomatoes, and bell peppers, can be included too. Using herbs or **marinating** the meat by soaking it in a sauce beforehand give shish kebabs a delicious flavor.

Equipment

- Skewers (wooden or metal)
- Container to soak skewers in (if using wooden skewers)
- Medium-size bowl
- Wooden spoon
- Cutting board

Ingredients

- 1 clove of garlic, finely chopped
- A few sprigs of rosemary or mint, finely chopped
- 1 pound of lean lamb, diced
- 1 pound of your favorite vegetables (try bell peppers, onions, tomatoes, and mushrooms), cut into pieces
- 3 cups of cooked rice

What to Do

1. If you're using wooden skewers, soak them in water for about 20 minutes to prevent them from burning when the kebabs are cooking.

2. Add the garlic and herbs to the lamb in the bowl and mix thoroughly. Let the lamb absorb the flavors for at least 15 minutes.

3. Thread the lamb and vegetables on the skewers in a nice pattern.

Ask an adult for help with using the skewers and broiler.

4

Cook the kebabs quickly on high heat on the broiler for about 5 minutes, turning them once. Quick cooking seals the meat and keeps the flavor in. Shish kebabs can also be cooked on the barbecue or in a frying pan on the stove.

5

Check if the lamb is cooked by pricking one cube with a toothpick or skewer. If no colored juices run out, the lamb is cooked. Serve the shish kebabs with rice.

Let's Cook!

MAKES: 4 servings

PREPARATION TIME: 15 minutes

COOKING TIME: 20 minutes

FOOD VALUES: About 225 calories, 4 g of fat, 8 g of protein, and 40 g of carbohydrates per serving.

SPECIAL DIETS: Suitable for nut-free diets. For vegan and vegetarian diets, replace the chicken with nuts and use vegetable bouillon; for kosher and halal diets, use certified meat; and for gluten-free diets, use couscous made from barley or other gluten-free grains.

What to Do

Chicken with Couscous

Couscous is a quick, simple, and healthy alternative to rice. Couscous is very popular in the North African countries of Morocco and Algeria, which many consider part of the Middle East. Couscous consists of small, pearl-like grains of semolina with a little wheat flour and salt. It is usually cooked over a flavored broth in a special food steamer. Couscous is often served with meat or vegetable stews.

Equipment

- 2 medium-size bowls
- Tablespoon
- Small, sharp knife
- Cutting board
- Medium-size saucepan
- Fork
- Wooden spoon
- Frying pan
- Serving dish

Ingredients

- 1 teaspoon of ground cumin
- 1 teaspoon of ground coriander
- ½ teaspoon of grated ginger
- ½ teaspoon of cinnamon
- A pinch of pepper
- 2 cloves of garlic, finely chopped
- 1 pound of skinless, boneless chicken breast fillets, diced
- 3 bell peppers (red, green, and yellow)
- 2½ cups of water
- 2 cubes of chicken bouillon
- 1 cup of couscous
- 4 scallions, chopped
- 2 teaspoons of olive oil
- Juice of 1 lime
- ¼ cup of dates (or raisins), chopped
- A handful of fresh cilantro, chopped
- 1 lemon, cut into wedges

Combine the ground cumin and coriander, ginger, cinnamon, pepper, and half of the garlic with the diced chicken in one bowl, making sure that the chicken is evenly covered with spices.

Wash the bell peppers, cut them in half, and discard the stems, seeds, and white pith. Cut the bell peppers into pieces about ¼ inch square.

Add the water to the saucepan, along with crumbled cubes of chicken bouillon. Stir the bouillon over medium heat until near boiling. Carefully set aside half a cup of bouillon, then add the couscous to the saucepan. Take the saucepan off the stove and leave the couscous to absorb the liquid (about 5 minutes), then fluff it lightly with a fork. Set it aside.

22

How To: Sauté

Heat the oil on high, then add the chopped vegetables. Stir the vegetables frequently so that each piece cooks evenly. Cook until lightly browned.

Recipe Variations

Replace the water with orange and lemon juice flavored with honey and cinnamon. Add ½ cup of chopped apricots, a crushed clove of garlic, some chopped mint, and ¼ cup of raisins instead of chicken.

4

Gently **sauté** the rest of the garlic, bell peppers, and scallions in the frying pan with the olive oil. Transfer to the clean bowl.

5

Add the spiced chicken pieces, lime juice, and a little hot chicken bouillon to the frying pan and gently simmer until cooked (about 5–7 minutes).

6

Add the sautéed vegetables, chopped dates, and the rest of the bouillon to the frying pan. Stir the cilantro gently into the mixture.

7

Transfer the couscous to a serving dish and top with the chicken and sautéed vegetables. Pour any remaining chicken bouillon over the dish. Garnish with lemon wedges.

Orange *Sharbat*

Sharbat is one of the most widespread Middle Eastern drinks. It came originally from Persia (an old name for Iran) as a rare treat made from fruit syrup, honey, and snow, and was popular in Ottoman Turkey. Try this on a hot day!

MAKES: 2 servings

PREPARATION TIME: 15 minutes

FOOD VALUES: About 340 calories, 8 g of fat, 6 g of protein, and 82 g of carbohydrates per glass.

SPECIAL DIETS: Suitable for vegan, vegetarian, nut-free, gluten-free, kosher, and halal diets.

Equipment

- Cutting board
- Small, sharp knife
- Citrus juicer
- Pitcher
- Measuring spoons
- Wooden spoon
- Measuring cup
- 2 tall glasses

Ingredients

- 8 medium-size oranges
- White sugar, to taste
- ½ teaspoon of orange blossom water
- Cold water
- Ice cubes
- 2 sprigs of fresh mint

What to Do

1 Roll the oranges on the cutting board with the palm of your hand, pressing down hard to free the juice inside.

2 Cut each orange in half and squeeze the juice out with the citrus juicer. Pour the juice into the pitcher.

3 Sweeten the juice with a little sugar if necessary.

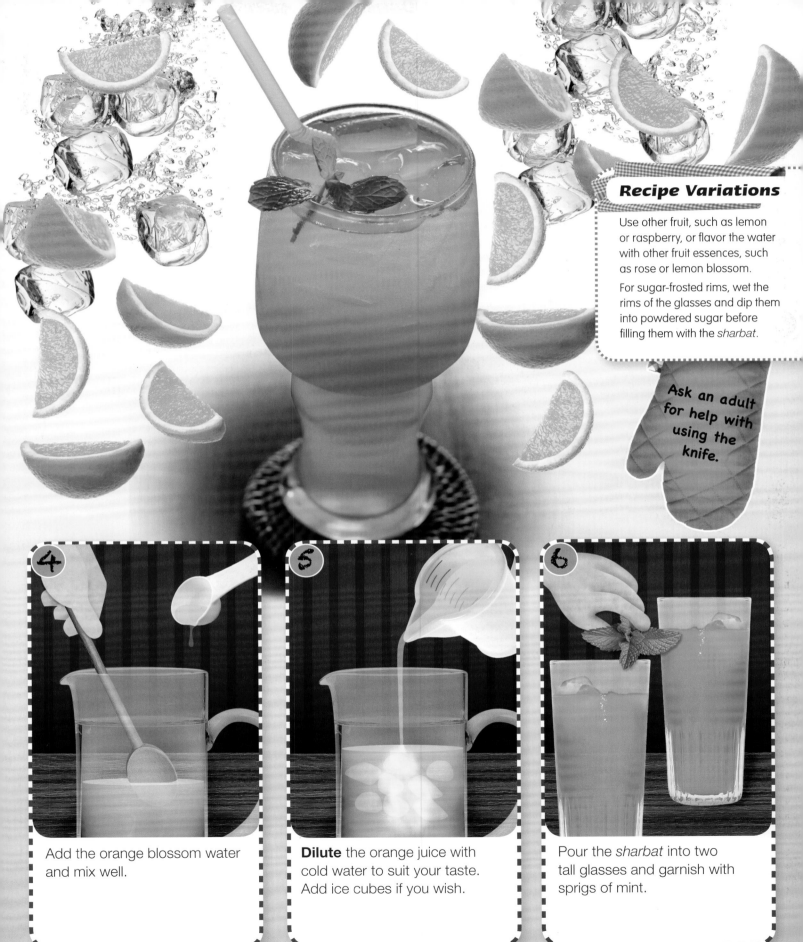

Recipe Variations

Use other fruit, such as lemon or raspberry, or flavor the water with other fruit essences, such as rose or lemon blossom.

For sugar-frosted rims, wet the rims of the glasses and dip them into powdered sugar before filling them with the *sharbat*.

Ask an adult for help with using the knife.

4 Add the orange blossom water and mix well.

5 **Dilute** the orange juice with cold water to suit your taste. Add ice cubes if you wish.

6 Pour the *sharbat* into two tall glasses and garnish with sprigs of mint.

Turkish Delight

Turkish delight is a soft, sticky sweet that was first made by a confectioner in Istanbul, Turkey, in 1777 CE. His family firm is still producing it from the same shop today. The simplest Turkish delight is made from corn flour, sugar, and flavorings. However, it may also include chopped dates and nuts, such as pistachios and hazelnuts.

MAKES: 20 pieces

PREPARATION TIME: 1 hour

COOKING TIME: 16 minutes

FOOD VALUES: About 63 calories and 15 g of carbohydrates per piece. No fat or protein.

SPECIAL DIETS: Suitable for vegan, vegetarian, nut-free, gluten-free, kosher, and halal diets.

Equipment

- Large microwave-safe bowl
- Wooden spoon
- Measuring cup
- Oven mitts
- Baking pan (7 inches x 11 inches), lightly greased
- Butter knife
- Airtight container

Ingredients

- 2 cups of superfine sugar
- 2 tablespoons of corn flour
- 1 teaspoon of cream of tartar
- 1 cup of water
- ½ teaspoon of rose water
- 1–2 drops of red food coloring
- ½ cup of powdered sugar

What to Do

1 Combine the superfine sugar, corn flour, cream of tartar, and water in the large microwave-safe bowl.

2 Microwave on high, uncovered, for about 7 minutes. Stir well and microwave on high for another 7 minutes. If it is still runny, stir again and microwave on high for up to 2 minutes.

3 Using a pair of oven mitts, carefully remove the bowl from the microwave. Next, stir in the rose water and food coloring.

Recipe Variations

Include ½ cup of your favorite chopped nuts, such as hazelnuts or almonds, when you add the rose water and food coloring.

Instead of rose water, try using lemon or mint essences.

Ask an adult for help with using the microwave and knife.

4

When cool, transfer the mixture to the baking pan and refrigerate until it is firm.

5

Cut the firm Turkish delight into cubes using a wet butter knife.

6

Sprinkle powdered sugar over the cubes and toss to coat them evenly. Transfer the cubes to an airtight container and store in the refrigerator until you're ready to serve them.

27

A Middle Eastern Food Celebration: Eid-ul-Fitr

This Muslim festival is an annual holiday celebrating the end of the month-long fast of Ramadan, when Muslims do not eat between sunrise and sunset. It is celebrated all over the Middle East, where most countries are Muslim.

What Is Eid-ul-Fitr?

During the month of Ramadan, Muslims pray and fast, honoring the Prophet Mohammed's gift of sacred knowledge in 610 CE. They also fast to understand what it is like to not have enough to eat. Eid-ul-Fitr means "celebration at the end of the fast."

How Is Eid-ul-Fitr celebrated?

This festival involves three days of feasting and celebrations. Muslims often wear new clothes on Eid-ul-Fitr. Early on the first morning, they eat a sweet or dates to break their fast and go to a service at a mosque. After this, they join their families to celebrate with special feasts. They also donate food or money to the poor. Adults often give children gifts of money or sweets, and contact friends and family to wish them well. People are encouraged to forget any grudges they have held during the year. Whole communities may also celebrate with meals together.

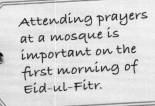

Attending prayers at a mosque is important on the first morning of Eid-ul-Fitr.

Egyptian Muslims share a meal in a Cairo neighborhood to celebrate breaking their fast.

Food

Feasting is a vital part of Eid-ul-Fitr. Muslims in different countries cook their own favorite dishes. In Middle Eastern countries this may be *biryani*, a dish of rice layered with a thick, intensely flavored meat or vegetable sauce. Special cookies and sweets are also eaten to celebrate Eid-ul-Fitr in many countries. These include the Egyptian *kahk*, which is a cookie filled with nuts and covered with sugar, and the Iraqi national cookie called *klaicha*, which is flavored with rose water and cardamom, and often filled with dates. Traditional sweets, such as Turkish delight and baklava, are often given to children who visit door-to-door.

Special treats are available for Eid-ul-Fitr in all Muslim countries.

Try This!

Cooking is a creative skill you can enjoy every day. Try these activities and learn more about cooking Middle Eastern food.

- Find out more about the Muslim month of fasting, known as Ramadan, and the foods associated with it, such as dates.

- Plan a trip around the Middle East to eat all of your favorite Middle Eastern foods. Where would you go first?

- Visit your nearest Middle Eastern grocery store and buy an interesting ingredient to cook with.

- Plant some parsley, cilantro, and mint so you can use fresh herbs in your Middle Eastern cooking.

- Find out more about one of the ancient civilizations of the Middle East. What foods from that civilization do we still eat?

- Collect some Middle Eastern dishes on which to serve your Middle Eastern foods. Which foods would suit each dish?

- Find your local Middle Eastern restaurant and pay it a visit. What is your favorite dish there?

- What are the main spices used in Middle Eastern cooking? Create a booklet with pictures of these spices along with a list of dishes in which they are used.

Glossary

allergic
having an allergy, or a bad reaction to certain foods

calories
units measuring the amount of energy food provides

carbohydrates
substances that provide the body with energy

civilizations
the cultures or ways of life of certain societies or countries during a period of time

climate
the general weather conditions of an area

culture
the ways of living that a group of people has developed over time

diets
foods and drinks normally consumed by different people or groups of people

dilute
make weaker by adding water

economy
the system of trade by which a country makes and uses its wealth

empires
groups of countries or peoples ruled by emperors or other powerful heads of state or governments

fertile
capable of producing good crops

garnish
use a small amount of a certain food to add flavor or color to a dish

gluten
a protein found in wheat and some other grains that makes dough springy

Jews
people who follow the religion of Judaism

marinating
soaking in a mixture of herbs, oils, and spices to add flavor to food

migrated
moved from one country to another to live permanently

Muslim
a person who follows the religion of Islam

native
living or growing naturally in a place

nutritious
providing nutrients, or nourishment

protein
a nutrient that helps bodies grow and heal

staple foods
foods that are eaten regularly and are the main parts of a diet

traditions
patterns of behavior handed down through generations

Index